Remembering the Fallen of the Great War at Christ Church

Natalie Bass

Christ Church Welshpool

Published in 2022 by Christ Church Welshpool
ISBN: 978-1-3999-4386-4

Printed by Welshpool Printing Group

Walking through the churchyard each day, different things catch my eye particularly the inscriptions on the headstones. I often find myself pausing and wondering about the lives and stories behind these names carved in stone. It slowly dawned on me that there were several headstones in the churchyard that commemorated someone that had died whilst serving in the First World War. Phrases such as 'missing in France'... 'killed in action in Sulva Bay'... 'buried near Baghdad'... made me curious about the lives of these men, whose brave actions were hinted at on their family tombstones. It also made me realise my own lack of knowledge about the First World War... where indeed was Sulva Bay and why were British forces fighting in Baghdad 100 years ago?

The centenary of the Great War was a good prompt for me to find out more about the stories of these men, and to share them in an exhibition 'Remembering the Fallen of the Great War at Christ Church'. There are 29 memorials in the churchyard and within the church itself that have a dedication to someone who died in the First World War. On the centenary of their death, I displayed their story and placed a hand painted slate poppy next to their memorial.

Each of the men have a very different story to tell but they are all connected by being commemorated here at Christ Church. Their stories are fascinating and heart wrenching. Incredibly they highlight most of the key events and aspects of the Great War; these men from a small market town in Mid-Wales playing their part in major world events.

Their stories also give a glimpse of what life was like in Welshpool and Montgomeryshire 100 years ago, especially as many of the houses the men grew up in are now no longer standing. Several of the stories are connected through family ties or through their work. Some were Welshpool men born and bred, several moved to Welshpool in childhood, while others came to Welshpool after they had enlisted to train with the Montgomeryshire Yeomanry. Several of the men are buried here, but most are buried overseas where they fell. Tragically some have no known grave.

Many of the men grew up together and went off to war together. The Great War involved a whole generation from all walks of life, from aristocracy to farmers, university students to grocers. Some families were hit particularly hard with the loss of two sons. It must have been an incredibly difficult and heart-wrenching time for the entire community.

Since displaying the stories in the Remembering the Fallen of the Great War at Christ Church exhibition, the response from people has been incredibly supportive and encouraging. It was felt that a fitting culmination of the project would be to bring the stories all together in the publication of a book. I hope that you find it as fascinating a read as I did researching it. As the headstones in the churchyard slowly weather and become enveloped in ivy, it seems even more important to honour the memory of these brave men.

Contents

William Quinn

Private :: South Wales Borderers

Killed in Action :: 31st October 1914 :: France & Flanders

The memorial in the churchyard reads:

Also of Pte. William M. Quinn 1st S.W.B.

Youngest son of J. and E. Quinn

Who was killed in action at Landreices

Oct 31st 1914. Aged 34 years.

'Faithful unto death'

William Quinn was born in Welshpool and was the son of John and Elizabeth Quinn. He was the youngest of their four children. His father John originated from Ireland and was a French polisher by trade. William's mother Elizabeth was from Berriew. The family lived in 10 Bear Yard, Brook Street. The house is no longer standing as this area of 'The Back Road' has been developed and is now the former Sainsbury's car park.

Site of Bear Yard, Brook Street.

There appears to be some discrepancy as to William's year of birth. The gravestone here at Christ Church states that he was 34 when he died in 1914, making his year of birth 1880. However, both the 1881 and 1891 census indicate his year of birth to be 1877.

At the age of 14, in 1891, William was working as an errand boy.

William became a soldier several years before the Great War. As a young man in his twenties and whilst in Manchester, William enlisted with the South Wales Borderers and was drafted to India. In 1911 he was stationed at Chatham Barracks in Kent.

At the outbreak of war on 4th August 1914, the first battalion of the South Wales Borderers were mobilised. After several days of preparation, they travelled by train to Southampton. On 12th August William's battalion left Britain to sail across the Channel to La Havre. On arrival, they made their way through Northern France towards Belgium. The battalion formed part of the British Expeditionary Force to prevent the German Army continuing their advance into France and Belgium.

A few weeks later, in the middle of September, the battalion was involved in armed combat during the Battle of Aisne. It was during these first few weeks of the war that the German Army discovered 'trench warfare' – where a position could be held even when your men are exhausted. This helped shape the rest of the war as the front line rapidly became static.

Both armies wanted to secure the coastal ports. The Allies tried to outflank the Germans at Ypres and the South Wales Borderers were involved in the First Battle of Ypres.

William was killed in action on 31st October 1914, at Landrecies, in Northern France. He was 34 years old.

William is commemorated on the Menin Gate, Ypres memorial, which is a memorial dedicated to the Missing who have no known grave.

Having lived in Manchester, William is commemorated on a war memorial in St. Clements Church, Ordsall, Manchester.

He is also commemorated on the Welshpool War Memorial.

'Faithful unto death'

2

William David Edwards

Lance Corporal :: Montgomeryshire Yeomanry

Died :: 21st May 1915 :: UK

The memorial in the churchyard reads:

Known to be buried in this churchyard

2636 Lance Cpl

W. D. Edwards

Montgomeryshire Yeomanry

21st May 1915

William David Edwards was born in Welshpool in 1882. He was the eldest son of William and Jane Edwards. His father William was a shoemaker and originated from Rhayader. The family lived at 16 Gungrog Terrace. When William was 19, he was working as a tailor. William married Mary, who originated from Cardigan, and they had two daughters, Margaret and Winifred. They moved house several times living in 1 Abbey Terrace, Waterloo Shop on Salop Road, 1 Mill Place, then back to Waterloo Shop. He continued to work as a tailor throughout this time.

William enlisted with the Montgomeryshire Yeomanry, but very little information on his military service can be found. This may be because a significant amount of WW1 military records were destroyed by fire during WW2.

William died in 1915 whilst he was residing at Waterloo Shop. He was 33 years old. The cause of death isn't known. He was buried in Welshpool.

Waterloo Shop, Salop Road.

William's Portland headstone sits alongside the drive and has often been a point of interest within the churchyard as it reads 'Known to be buried within this churchyard'. It seems that a plan of the burials within the churchyard was not kept, and the location of his grave has been forgotten over time.

As there is a graveyard at both St Mary's Parish Church and here at Christ Church, the parish burial records have a 'C.C.' inscribed in the margin for a Christ Church burial. However, there is no such inscription by William Edwards' name.

In 1960 the Area Superintendent of the Commonwealth War Graves Commission asked the Church Warden if they knew the location of William Edward's grave. On enquiring with the local Old Comrades of the Montgomeryshire Yeomanry, a member recalls being a bearer at William's funeral. Unfortunately he could not remember the exact location of the grave, but he thought that it was at Christ Church.

It would appear that on this evidence alone the headstone was erected here at Christ Church by the Commonwealth War Graves Commission in 1961. To distinguish the plot as not containing a burial, the headstone was positioned facing west rather than to the east, as is the norm, and placed in an area that is clearly too small for a burial.

3
Leonard Augustus Hedge

Lance Corporal :: Montgomeryshire Yeomanry

Accidental Death :: 16th June 1915 :: UK

The memorial in the churchyard reads:

In loving memory of

Leonard Augustus Hedge

Lance Corporal Dispatch Rider 2/1st Montgomery Yeomanry

Born June 14th 1887   Died June 16th 1915

Leonard Augustus Hedge was born on 14th June 1887 in Shelton, Stoke-on-Trent. He was the third son of George and Mary Hedge. His father George was a brewer. Leonard was educated at Dean Close School, a private boarding school in Cheltenham.

In the 1911 census, Leonard is recorded as living in Uttoxeter, Staffordshire, working as a bank clerk.

When war broke out in August 1914, Leonard was a senior bank clerk at the United Counties Bank in Brecon.

The site of the United Counties Bank, Brecon

While living in Brecon, Leonard was described as being a popular member of the community and was an active sportsman. Not long before he enlisted, he helped to rescue a man from drowning in the River Usk.

With the outbreak of war, Leonard travelled to Welshpool on 20th September 1914 to enlist with the Montgomeryshire Yeomanry. The 2/1st Montgomeryshire Yeomanry was formed in September 1914 as a second line regiment and remained at home during the war. The regimental headquarters were in Welshpool.

Leonard Augustus Hedge.

Leonard was in training to become a Motorcycle Dispatch Rider. On 16th June 1915, he was promoted to Corporal. Later that evening, as he rode through Llanymynech, he collided with a lorry carrying mineral water and died minutes later. It was thought that a large tree in the village obscured the lights of the lorry as Leonard was traveling down a hill.

He died just two days after his 28th birthday.

Leonard is commemorated on the Montgomeryshire Yeomanry memorial inside St. Mary's Church, Welshpool. However, an error has resulted in 'Armstrong' cited as his middle name, rather than Augustus.

Montgomeryshire Yeomanry memorial plaque.

Leonard is commemorated on the Brecon War Memorial.

Brecon War Memorial.

At Dean Close School in Cheltenham, a chapel was built in the school grounds in 1923, as a memorial to the 120 past pupils who died in the Great War.

Leonard was buried in the churchyard here at Christ Church with full military honours.

4

David Charles Sapple

Private :: Royal Welsh Fusiliers

Killed in Action :: 10th August 1915 :: Gallipoli

The memorial in the churchyard reads:

Also of their second son,

David Charles

Who was killed at Gallipoli

August 10th 1915   Aged 17 years

'Greater love hath no man than this that

A man lay down his life for his friends.'

David Charles Sapple was born in Newtown in 1898 and was the son of Richard and Mary Sapple, who both originated from Welshpool. The family lived at Jack Street, Turners Court, Newtown. His father Richard was a poultry dealer. His mother Mary was a sister to William Waring VC (story no. 25).

When Charles was very young, the family moved to Welshpool to live at 5 Mount Place, which was on the corner of Mount Street and Chapel Street. The house is no longer standing.

Mount Place was a row of small houses sited where the shed and wooden fence are now, on the corner of Mount Street and Chapel Street.

The family lived at Mount Place for over 10 years before moving just around the corner to Park House, 1 Chapel Street.

Park House, 1 Chapel Street.

Whilst Charles was still a teenager, he enlisted with the 7th Battalion (Montgomeryshire) Royal Welsh Fusiliers.

The 1/7th RWF were a territorial force, which in 1914 were based in Newtown as part of the North Wales Brigade of the Welsh Division. During training the battalion moved to Conway, followed by Northampton and later Cambridge, before moving to Bedford in May 1915. At this time the battalion became part of the 158th Brigade of the 53rd Division.

David Charles Sapple.

As the First World War progressed into 1915, other countries became involved in the conflict. Turkey joined the Central Powers of Germany and Austria – Hungary. Hoping to break the deadlock on the Western Front, Britain and France decided to deploy troops to fight Germany's new ally, Turkey. It was hoped that Germany would be forced to divert troops from the Western Front to support Turkey, as well as creating an opportunity to secure a supply route to Russia.

The campaign in Gallipoli, a peninsula in Turkey, began in April 1915. The Turks had been dismissed as an inferior force which was soon proved to be very inaccurate. After British, French, Australian and New Zealand troops landed, conditions on the Gallipoli Peninsula soon became very tough, rivalling the trenches on the Western Front. Both sides dug in whilst having to face high temperatures with no shade, on rock-hard ground. It didn't take long for troops to fall to disease, inaction and hopeless assaults.

Almost three months passed before the British government attempted to break the deadlock by sending another five divisions, while the Turks sent fifteen.

15,000 Allied troops were sent to a new landing north of Anzac Cove, called Sulva Bay. The 1/7th RWF in the 53rd Division were part of this new attack.

On 19th July 1915, Charles along with his battalion, embarked on a HM Transport Ship in Devonport, Plymouth and sailed for Gallipoli. They landed at Sulva Bay on 9th August. The battalion's first action of the war was on the following day, when they had to cross the dry Salt Lake at Sulva to take Scimitar Hill. Unfortunately, the chain of command during the Sulva Bay attack broke down and it consequently failed. Conditions were poor due to smoke from the burning scrub and chaos soon ensued. Many of the men were never seen again, including Charles. He was killed in action at the age of 17.

Welshpool lost at least three men in the Sulva Bay attack on the 10th August. John Williams (story no. 5) also died that day, and John Holloway (story no. 6) was fatally wounded. All three grew up within a stone's throw of each other in the shadow of Christ Church.

Charles' body was never found. He is commemorated on the Helles Memorial, which stands on the tip of the Gallipoli Peninsula.

Charles is also commemorated on both the Welshpool War Memorial and Newtown War Memorial.

A bronze 'Next of Kin Memorial Plaque' or 'Death Penny' was produced by the British Government from December 1918 for the next of kin of all those who had lost their lives as a result of the First World War. It was a form of commemoration and acknowledgement of sacrifice. Each one had the name of the deceased soldier cast into the metal. No rank was included to show equality in their sacrifice. Charles Sapple's memorial plaque has been incorporated into the family headstone.

Charles Sapple's memorial plaque.

'Greater love hath no man than this that
A man lay down his life for his friends.'

5

John Pryce Williams

Private :: Royal Welsh Fusiliers

Killed in Action :: 10th August 1915 :: Gallipoli

The memorial in the churchyard reads:

Also of Pte John Williams 7th RWF

Younger son of John and Fanny Williams

Who was killed at Sulva Bay

August 10th 1915   Aged 22 Years

'Thy will be done'

John Pryce Williams was born in Pool Quay near Welshpool on 9th July 1893. He was the son of John and Fanny Williams and was their third child. His father originated from Llansaintffraid and his mother was from Kerry. The family lived at Swan Bank in Pool Quay. At the time of John's birth his father worked as a 'gentleman servant'.

By 1901 the family had moved to Welshpool and his father was working as a 'domestic gardener'. Ten years later, John's father had died, and the family were living at 19 Mount Street in the shadow of Christ Church. John was working as a postman.

19 Mount Street.

At the outbreak of war, John enlisted with the 1/7th (Montgomeryshire) Battalion of the Royal Welsh Fusiliers, a territorial force. From here on, John's story is very similar to his neighbour and comrade, Charles Sapple (previous story).

John set sail on 19th July 1915 from Devonport, Plymouth on a HM Transport Ship bound for Gallipoli. Three weeks later, on 9th August, he landed at Sulva Bay. The following day, in sweltering heat, John was part of the attack to take Scimitar Hill from the Turks. He had to cross

24

the dry Salt Lake and go into the hills through smoke and burning scrub. During this attack, John was killed in action. He was 22 years old. Many of the battalion's men died that day and the attack failed.

John's body was never found. He is commemorated on the Helles Memorial which stands at the tip of the Gallipoli Peninsula.

John is also commemorated on the Welshpool War Memorial.

'Thy will be done'

6

John Thomas Holloway

Private :: Royal Welsh Fusiliers

Died of Wounds :: 23rd August 1915 :: Malta

The memorial in the churchyards reads:

In loving memory of

Pte John Holloway 1/7th RWF

Son of William and Sarah Holloway

Wounded at Sulva Bay August 10th

And died at Malta August 23rd 1915

Aged 19 Years

'Thy will be done'

John Thomas Holloway was born in Welshpool in 1895. He was the son of William and Sarah Holloway and was the fourth of their nine children. Both William and Sarah originated from Welshpool. The family lived at 9 Whittington Passage. His father William was a painter (and incidentally painted the interior of Christ Church). By 1911 the family had moved to live at 21 Mount Street and later moved just up the road to 23 Mount Street. However, census information shows that in 1911 at aged 15, John was living at Plas-Y-Court Farm just outside Middletown (the farm next to the main road on the Wales - England border). He was working as a farm labourer. Sometime after this, John moved to South Wales to work in the coal mines.

Whittington Passage.

Whittington Passage runs parallel to Jehu Road, from the High Street (next to Andrew's Fish Bar) to Bowling Green Lane.

John returned home to enlist with the 2/7th (Montgomeryshire) Battalion of the Royal Welsh Fusiliers. He was soon transferred to 1/7th Montgomeryshire Battalion. From here John's story follows the same path as Charles Sapple and John Williams (previous two stories).

On 19th July 1915, John embarked on a HM Transport Ship at Devonport, Plymouth to sail to Gallipoli. Three weeks later, on 9th August, he landed at Sulva Bay. In awful heat, the battalion as part of the 53rd Division were ordered to advance to Simitar Hill. They had to cross the dry Salt Lake and go into the hills beyond through smoke and burning scrub.

John was wounded by a bullet in his stomach during this attack. He was put on a hospital ship bound for Malta for treatment.

PTE. JOHN HOLLOWAY, WELSHPOOL.

Malta became a hospital island in 1915 due to the battle fronts at Gallipoli in Turkey and Salonika in Greece requiring a place to treat the wounded at a safe distance behind the front line. The island became known as the 'Nurse of the Mediterranean'. The wounded soldiers had to make a weeklong journey across the Mediterranean on hospital ships, which was dangerous in itself as the ships had to avoid German submarines and mines. The cramped conditions on the ships for the wounded men meant that the risk of infectious disease was high.

John safely arrived in Malta and was treated for his injuries, but he died just days later, on 23rd August 1915. He was 19 years old.

John was buried at the Capuccini Naval Cemetery in Malta. He is commemorated on the Welshpool War Memorial.

'Thy will be done'

It is poignant that these three Welshpool boys, Charles Sapple, John Williams and John Holloway, who would have known each other from childhood, possibly played together on Mount Street, enlisted together, sailed to Gallipoli together, fought at Sulva Bay side by side... all died because of the events on that fateful day.

7

Ernest Watkins

Private :: Montgomeryshire Yeomanry

Died :: 8th March 1916 :: Ireland

The memorial in the churchyard reads:

Also of Ernest Watkins, Solicitor,

Their youngest son {John & Margaret Watkins}

Who died in Dublin whilst serving with the 3/1 Montgomeryshire Yeomanry,

March 8th 1916,

In his 34th year.

Ernest Watkins was born in 1882 in Welshpool. He was the youngest of John and Margaret Watkins' four children. His father John originated from Tregynon and was the manager of the coal wharf at the railway station for the J. & M. Morris Foundry. Margaret was from Berriew. The family lived at 4 New Street.

4 New Street.

When Ernest was a young man, his father died. Ernest continued to live with his mother and two of his sisters in New Street. He had a flourishing career as a Solicitors Articled Clerk and was deputy to the Town Clerk. He was also Secretary for Welshpool Golf Club, probably around the time the golf club moved from the Deer Park at Powis Castle to the 'windy common' at Red Bank (where the Guilsfield road and Windmill Lane meet. It has since moved again to its present location up on the Golfa). Ernest was also a member of the Freemasons.

Ernest was not a 'physically robust' man therefore clerical work suited him very well.

Ernest enlisted with the Montgomeryshire Yeomanry as a Clerk. The 3/1 regiment was raised in Welshpool in June 1915 as a new recruiting and depot regiment, as the 2/1 regiment had become a fighting unit.

The new 3/1 regiment quickly recruited up to 600 men. Leading it was Major Tamworth who took them to Ireland for the winter to progress their training. The brigade was housed in Marlborough Barracks in Dublin and later moved to Arbour Hill Barracks.

Only a month after enlisting, whilst undergoing 'arduous' outdoor training before taking up his clerical duties, Ernest contracted pneumonia. He was admitted to the Royal Military Hospital in Dublin, where he died on 8th March 1916. He was 34 years old. His body was returned to Welshpool, and he was buried here at Christ Church.

At the Freemasons headquarters in London, Ernest is commemorated in a memorial book housed in a sarcophagus.

Freemasons memorial book.

Ernest is also commemorated on a plaque in New Street United Church. The plaque was originally housed in the Congregational Church next door, where Ernest attended. His name is also listed on the Welshpool War Memorial, as well as on the Montgomeryshire Yeomanry memorial inside St. Mary's Church, Welshpool.

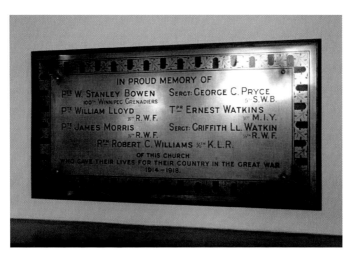

Congregational Church memorial plaque.

Montgomeryshire Yeomanry memorial plaque.

8

Maurice Edwin Weaver

Private :: 1st Herefordshire Regiment

Died :: 31st May 1916 :: UK

The memorial in the churchyard reads:

8197 Private

M E Weaver

Herefordshire Regiment

31st May 1916

Maurice Edwin Weaver was born in Montgomery in 1890. He went by the name of Edwin, which was also his father's name. His mother was Mary Jane, and he had two sisters, Susannah and Florence. His father worked as a mason. The family lived at Plough Bank on Pool Road in Montgomery. Shortly after he was born, in 1891, his father died. Two years later Edwin's mother Mary married John Evans, who was a navvy, a general labourer. The family moved to Rhayader and settled in Caeherbert Lane.

By 1911, at aged 21, Edwin was working at The Fleece Temperance Hotel in South Street, Rhayader. He held the position of 'boots', a hotel porter. The Fleece Temperance Hotel is no longer standing.

The Fleece Temperance Hotel, Rhayader.

On 11th February 1911, Edwin enlisted with the 1st Herefordshire Regiment which was a Territorial Force. He attended summer training camps for the following three years.

At the outbreak of war in August 1914, the battalion was instructed to go to Hereford to become part of the Welsh Border Brigade in the Welsh Division. On mobilisation they transferred to Pembroke Dock, but soon moved on to Oswestry. By December they were in Bury St

Edmunds. In May 1915 the regiment became part of the 158th Brigade in the 53rd Welsh Division and moved to Bedford.

Shortly after arriving in Bedford, Edwin was admitted to hospital with lumps in his groin. He was transferred to 1st Southern General Hospital in Birmingham for further treatment on the lymphatic abscesses, which included several operations. He was in hospital for nearly a year.

The 1st Southern General Hospital was a war hospital set up at the University in Edgbaston, Birmingham. The University buildings were given over as part of the war effort.

As his health deteriorated, Edwin was permanently discharged from the Army on 19th March 1916 due to 'total incapacity, not a result of but aggravated by ordinary Military Service'. Whilst still in hospital, Edwin developed Pulmonary Tuberculosis and it was noted that he had lost a lot of weight. He was discharged from hospital on 19th May 1916 and was transferred to The Beachwood House Hospital, a convalescent home in Newport, South Wales. Shortly afterwards, Edwin died on 31st May 1916. He was 26 years old.

Edwin was buried here at Christ Church. It isn't known why Edwin was buried here in Welshpool as opposed to Rhayader. Maybe it was because the family originated from the Welshpool area, but also Edwin's eldest sister Susannah lived in Welshpool so there were some family ties.

Meanwhile his battalion had sailed to Sulva Bay and fought in the ill-fated Gallipoli campaign and suffered heavy losses.

Edwin is commemorated on the Welshpool War Memorial as well as on 'The Clock' War Memorial in Rhayader.

The Clock War Memorial, Rhayader.

9

Joseph Ithel Jehu Davies

Lieutenant :: Royal Welsh Fusiliers

Killed in Action :: 3rd September 1916 :: France & Flanders

The memorial in the churchyard reads:

In proud and loving memory of Joseph Ithel Jehu Davies,
Lieutenant commanding his company 1st Batt. Royal Welsh Fusiliers,
third son of Joseph H. and Sarah E. Davies,
killed while gallantly leading his men at Ginchy (Somme) September
3rd 1916   Aged 22 years.

His body rests in Deville Wood British Cemetery, France

'O valiant heart, who to your glory came, through dust of conflict and
through battle flame, tranquil you lie, your knightly virtue proved, your
memory hallowed in the land you loved.'

Joseph Ithel Jehu Davies was born on 10th August 1894 in Welshpool. He was the youngest of Joseph and Sarah Davies' three sons. His elder brothers were Stanley and Gilbert (of Gilbert Davies Solicitors).

The Davies brothers: Stanley, Ithel, Gilbert.

The family lived at Ty Coch on the High Street, where his father Joseph ran his business as a tailor. Joseph originated from Welshpool and Sarah was from Porthmadog. Both Joseph and Sarah were JP's and Sarah was Welshpool's first lady Mayor.

Ty Coch, High Street.

Ithel was schooled at Welshpool Grammar and County Schools. He went on to study Agricultural Sciences at Armstrong College, Durham University where he was on course for first class honours. Armstrong College was located in Newcastle upon Tyne and later became Newcastle University.

Whilst at university, Ithel was the President of the Agricultural Students' Association and contributed to the college magazine.

Ithel was a fine sportsman and athlete. He was captain of the Welshpool County School Football Club and went on to become the captain of the university football and rugby teams, as well as being a member of the university boxing team. He was an accomplished athlete and local sprint champion. At Durham Varsity Sports he won the 100- and 250-yards races. He became the Secretary of the university's Athletic Association. Ithel was due to participate in the trials for the

Olympic Athletic team for the 1914 Berlin Games, which were subsequently cancelled due to the outbreak of war.

Ithel also enjoyed singing and music. He had a 'good and well-trained bass voice' and often gave concerts locally. At university he was a member of the choir at Trinity Presbyterian Church, Newcastle. He played the organ at Welshpool's Presbyterian Church on Mount Street. (The Presbyterian Church later closed and became the Bethal Chapel which also closed and has subsequently been converted into flats known as Bethal Chapel Apartments).

The former Presbyterian Church, now Bethal Chapel Apartments.

Whilst at Armstrong College, Ithel was a member of the University Officers' Training Corps, therefore when war broke out, he was able to gain a commission with the Royal Welsh Fusiliers in December 1914.

Joseph Ithel Jehu Davies.

Ithel was posted to France in October 1915 with the Royal Welsh Fusiliers as part of the 7th Division of the British Expeditionary Force in France and Flanders.

In the trenches, Ithel was highly regarded by his men and by his commanding officers and distinguished himself with his 'courage and coolness'. He however never mentioned these gallant acts in his letters home, but they have been documented by others. A comrade wrote to Ithel thanking him for saving his life; he wrote, 'I am sure if it had not been for you, I should have not got here [hospital] at all, for I would have died from loss of blood... I hope you will come through alright.'

Whilst in the trenches, Ithel was keen to keep himself busy and so he formed an Army choir of over 30 voices. He also wrote poetry including the following poem 'Les Heros', which he dedicated to his mother.

Les Heros

On the battle-scared plains of north France,
Are our heroes who never knew fear,
Their spirits buoyed up by the chance,
That the end of the conflict is near.

Their strong faith in their tryst ne'er grows dim,
Through the strife has been fierce and long,
For they know in the end they must win,
In the battle of Right against Wrong.

And often the tale has been told,
Of deeds that are noble and brave,
How many a hero lies cold,
Through trying a comrade to save.

Their deeds through the empire shall ring,
Long after the struggle shall cease,
And we of their glory will sing,
And think how their last rest is – Peace.

In July 1916 the 1st Battalion, Royal Welsh Fusiliers became involved in the Battle of the Somme, a battle still considered the bloodiest battle in the history of warfare.

Ithel took part in the beginning of the Battle of Ginchy. The French village of Ginchy had been converted by the German Army into a heavily defended fortress village. It was situated where six roads meet making it an important point on the German defensive line. By late summer Ginchy was a mass of shattered masonry and shell-holes.

On September 3rd, Ginchy became the key objective for the battalion and the 7th Division. They gained control of the village, only to lose it again during a German counterattack.

Ithel was not to survive the day. His actions were documented as:

'...he was given the command of his company...

...he was seen attacking four of the enemy single-handed...

...he killed three of them and as far as we know, was killed by the fourth...

...he died the death of a true soldier...

...he always did his duty as an officer and a gentleman and died in the execution of it...

...we all miss him greatly...'

Ithel died on 3rd September 1916 and was buried at Deville Wood War Cemetery, Longueval, France. He was 22 years old.

Ithel's headstone in Deville Wood War Cemetery, France.

For many years Ithel's military medals were on display at Welshpool High School on the wall of the Headmaster's Office.

Ithel's military medals.

Ithel is commemorated on the Welshpool War Memorial. He is also commemorated on a marble plaque that was originally mounted in the Presbyterian Church and is now housed in the New Street United Church.

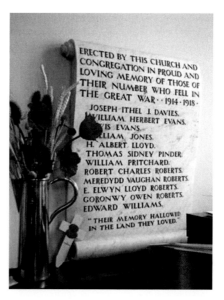

ERECTED BY THIS CHURCH AND CONGREGATION IN PROUD AND LOVING MEMORY OF THOSE OF THEIR NUMBER WHO FELL IN THE GREAT WAR · · 1914 · 1918 ·

JOSEPH ITHEL J. DAVIES.
WILLIAM HERBERT EVANS.
⸺IS EVANS.
⸺LLIAM JONES.
H. ALBERT LLOYD.
THOMAS SIDNEY PINDER.
WILLIAM PRITCHARD.
ROBERT CHARLES ROBERTS.
MEREDYDD VAUGHAN ROBERTS.
E. ELWYN LLOYD ROBERTS.
GORONWY OWEN ROBERTS.
EDWARD WILLIAMS.

"THEIR MEMORY HALLOWED IN THE LAND THEY LOVED."

Plaque inside New Street United Church.

Ithel's name joins a long list of 223 past Armstrong students who fell in the Great War on a large marble memorial plaque in the foyer of Armstrong College, now Newcastle University.

On the family tomb in the churchyard here at Christ Church, the sword on the west face of the headstone commemorates Ithel.

'In short measure
Life may perfect be'

10

Edwin Morris

Sergeant :: 1st Canadian Cavalry

Died of Wounds :: 5th October 1916 :: France & Flanders

The memorial in the churchyard reads:

In memory of Edwin, his {William Morris} son,
who gave his life for his country in France.

Oct 5th 1916   Aged 34 years.

Edwin Morris was born on 30th September 1881 in Welshpool. He was the 12th child of 17 children to William and Jane Morris. His father William was one of the industrious Morris brothers, (two of whom were the Foundry owners J. & M. Morris mentioned in story no. 20). William was a draper who had his shop in Broad Street (where Costa's is today). William also owned a flannel mill alongside the canal, just off Salop Road.

The family lived in Severn Villa situated on the other side of the canal to the flannel mill, on present day Little Henfaes Drive. This would have been a substantial house to accommodate the family and their servants. The house no longer stands and all that remains is a stone boundary wall and evidence of an entrance to the property flanking the canal.

An old entrance to Severn Villa.

The old boundary wall of Severn Villa adjacent to the canal.

The census of 1901 lists 19-year-old Edwin as living at Severn Villa, with his parents along with nine of his brothers and sisters. He was working as a mechanical engineer.

Sometime after this, Edwin emigrated to Canada. He settled in Alberta, working as a 'saw-fitter'. Edwin enlisted with the 19th Alberta Dragoons, a militia cavalry unit created in 1908, based in Edmonton.

At the outbreak of war, Canada assembled an Expeditionary Force at the request of Lord Kitchener. A hastily prepared training camp was set up in Valcartier, just outside Quebec City. Edwin enlisted with the Canadian Expeditionary Force in Valcartier on 23rd September 1914 and was given the rank of Sergeant.

Most of the Canadians who enlisted at the beginning of the war were British born. When all the militia's gathered at Valcartier from across Canada the camp held over 35,000 troops.

On 1st October 1914, Edwin as part of the 1st Canadian Cavalry Division embarked on the HMS Arcadian for a two-week voyage to England.

They arrived in Devonport, Plymouth on 15th October. The Division travelled by rail to Salisbury Plain where they trained for four months, mostly in deep mud as it was an exceptionally wet winter.

The Division was posted to France on 12th February 1915. It is likely that during the following 18 months Edwin was involved in several battles along the Western Front, which then culminated in the Battle of the Somme. At the beginning of October, the Division took part in The Battle of Le Transloy and The Battle of the Ancre Heights.

Edwin was wounded during heavy fighting and was taken to a hospital camp in Etaples. It was here that Edwin died on 5th October 1916, just days after his 35th birthday.

Edwin was buried at Etaples Military Cemetery. He is commemorated on the Welshpool War Memorial.

Situated near the south door inside Christ Church is a brass plaque erected by Edwin's Mother, sisters and brothers in memory of both Edwin and his brother Charles, who died in the Great War a short time later (story no. 16).

Brass plaque situated inside Christ Church.

The Morris family plot.

11

Percy Robert, Viscount Clive

Captain :: Welsh Guards

Died of Wounds :: 13th October 1916 :: UK

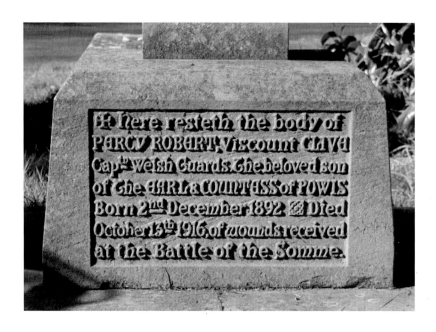

The memorial in the churchyard reads:

Here resteth the body of Percy Robert, Viscount Clive

Captain Welsh Guards,

The beloved son of the Earl & Countess of Powis

Born 2nd December 1892

Died October 13th 1916, of wounds received at the Battle of the Somme.

Percy Robert Herbert was born into a life of privilege and aristocracy being the first child of the 4th Earl of Powis, George Herbert and the Countess of Powis, Lady Violet. He was born on 2nd December 1892 at the Powis' London residence in Berkeley Square in Westminster. He inherited the title Viscount Clive as he was the new heir to the Powis Estate. His birth prompted much rejoicing throughout Powys and Shropshire. When Percy was brought home to Powis Castle in January 1893, there were celebrations in Powis Park lasting several days involving over 3000 people. Even snow on the ground didn't deter people from joining in the celebrations.

Percy was later joined by a sister, Hermione and a brother, Mervyn.

Powis Castle.

Percy was christened in St. George's Church in Hanover Square, Westminster. The young Viscount Clive was educated at Eton College and Sandhurst. Percy was described as having a 'courteous disposition and gentle demeanour'. He loved outdoor sports, particularly cricket and was a popular member of the Welshpool and Montgomeryshire teams. He also loved polo and hunting.

Percy joined the Army in October 1913 and became a Lieutenant with the Scots Guards. He was involved in the early part of the war in France during the autumn and winter of 1914. He was invalided home just before Christmas as he was suffering with frostbitten feet.

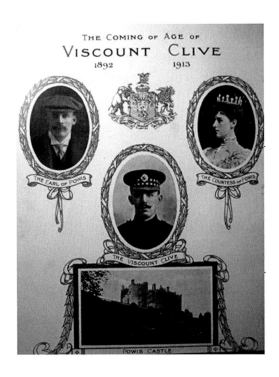

When he had recovered, he was transferred to the newly formed Welsh Guards, raised by King George V in February 1915. Percy was heavily involved in its early recruitment. The Battalion mounted its first King's Guard on 1st March 1915, St David's Day.

Percy - second from left, second row from the top.

On 17th August 1915, Percy returned to France for his second round of active service on the Western Front. With the Welsh Guards he was involved in heavy fighting in the Battle of Loos and the Battle of the Somme.

On 16th September 1916, during the offensive at Flers-Courcellette, Percy was hit in the right thigh by a German machine gun bullet. The bullet badly fractured his femur and remained lodged in his leg. He rolled into a disused German trench at Les Boeufs and lay there injured for several hours. He eventually received medical assistance and was taken to a hospital camp at Rouen. Whilst convalescing he wrote to his mother saying that he was fine and 'in no pain'.

The family arranged for Percy to be urgently transported home for further treatment. He underwent three operations at the King Edward VII Hospital, Grosvenor Gardens, London. It was noted that while he was undergoing treatment he never complained and showed a great deal of courage. After the bullet had been removed, Percy suffered severe haemorrhaging and blood poisoning. He died on 13th October 1916. He was 23 years old.

The Llangollen Advertiser published a very detailed account of Percy's funeral, showing the significance of the event. Percy's body was taken from King Edward VII's Hospital to the family home at Berkeley Square. The coffin was draped in a Union Jack with Percy's cap and sword laid on top. A gun carriage carried Percy through the West End to Paddington Station escorted by a detachment of Welsh Guards and eight drummers and accompanied by the Earl and Countess. They boarded the train to bring Percy's body to Welshpool.

At Welshpool train station a large crowd had gathered, and a gun carriage and six black horses waited in Station Square.

The Band of the King's Shropshire Light Infantry played Beethoven's Funeral March as it headed the cortege through the town and up to Christ Church. Laid on the coffin was a large laurel wreath bound with red and blue ribbon from the men of the Welsh Guards and a large floral tribute from the Scots Guards.

Lord Powis walked alone behind the gun carriage, followed by the estate managers, the chief constable and his deputy, Lieutenant Menzies and Private Lloyd (Percy's orderly). The Countess accompanied by her sister had gone ahead to Christ Church.

As the cortege made its way slowly through the centre of Welshpool, the streets were lined with mournful onlookers, and it was a very moving scene.

The Vicar and choir met the cortege at the churchyard gates. By the wishes of the Earl and Countess the general public were excluded from the churchyard, as they wanted a simple private service on the eve of his interment. Percy's coffin was carried into Christ Church on a bier and placed at the foot of the alter steps. A short service followed.

After the service the Earl and Countess stayed behind in the church for some time. They left the church and walked out of their private entrance to the churchyard up to Powis Castle before travelling to Walcot.

Percy's coffin remained in the church overnight and estate workmen kept watch throughout the night.

The interior of Christ Church.

Reflecting the sad mood of the town, the weather on the day of the interment was overcast with persistent rain. The flag was flown at half-mast and all business within Welshpool was suspended during the funeral service. Windows were shuttered and blinds were drawn as a mark of respect.

The grave which is situated alongside the church, was bricked and the sides were decorated with moss, studded with deep red and pure white dahlias.

The tenants of the Powis estates in Powys and Shropshire, the townspeople and many others gathered at Christ Church for the service. The building was described as 'quite inadequate' to accommodate so many mourners.

There were many floral tributes laid on the apse steps and against the choir stalls and the church was filled with their scent.

After the service, which was led by the Bishop, Percy's coffin was carried out of the church by members of the Welsh Guards. Around the grave a cordon was drawn for the chief mourners by the firing party which consisted of 100 members of the King's Shropshire Light Infantry. The graveside service was conducted in the pouring rain. The firing party discharged three volleys over the grave and the 'Last Post' was played by buglers from the Welsh Guards.

Ung je serviray

One will I serve

Audacter et sincere

Boldly and sincerely

Percy is commemorated on the Welshpool War Memorial. He is also commemorated on the House of Lords Royal Gallery Memorial in London.

Situated in what is known as 'the Powis corner' in Christ Church is a stained-glass window erected in memory of Percy, Viscount Clive by the Lymore Tenantry. The window depicts St George from a painting by Italian painter Andrea Mantegna (1431 – 1506) and includes the Powis crest and emblems of both the Welsh Guards and Scots Guards.

The window was dedicated by the Archbishop of Wales in September 1920.

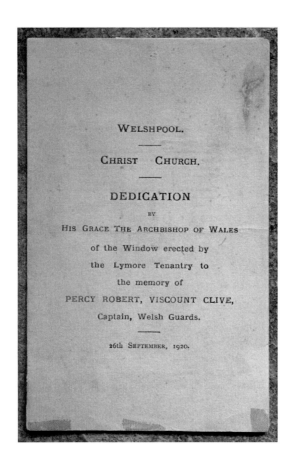

WELSHPOOL.

CHRIST CHURCH.

DEDICATION
BY

HIS GRACE THE ARCHBISHOP OF WALES

of the Window erected by

the Lymore Tenantry to

the memory of

PERCY ROBERT, VISCOUNT CLIVE,

Captain, Welsh Guards.

26th SEPTEMBER, 1920.

Order of service for the Dedication of the memorial window.

Percy's memorial window inside Christ Church.

12

John Thomas

Gunner :: Royal Garrison Artillery

Died :: 10th December 1916 :: Balkans

The memorial in the churchyard reads:

And of their {William & Elizabeth} sons,

John and Edward,

Who fell in the Great War.

R. I. P.

John 'Jack' Thomas was born in Welshpool on 20th August 1892. He was the son of William and Elizabeth Thomas. They had nine children but three died in infancy. Jack's father William originated from Meifod and was a labourer. His mother Elizabeth was from Llanfair Caereinion. The family lived at 47 Lledan Crescent on the 'Back Road', Brook Street. The house is no longer standing but it was situated where the former Library building is.

The site of Lledan Crescent.

Jack is described as tall with brown eyes and dark brown hair. He followed in his father's footsteps and worked as a labourer. During this time, he was a member of the Montgomeryshire Yeomanry, the local territorial militia.

It seems likely that Jack moved to the Crewe area, possibly seeking labouring work.

John Thomas, right, with his brother Edward.

Shortly after the outbreak of war, on 14th August 1914, Jack enlisted at Crewe. It was just days before his 21st birthday. He was given the position of Gunner in the 13th Heavy Battery, Royal Garrison Artillery.

The Royal Garrison Artillery manned the heavy siege guns, such as Howitzers with up to a 9" bore and the '60 Pounder' heavy field gun. The 13th Heavy Battery were raised as part of Kitchener's First New Army. The Division assembled on Salisbury Plain in August 1914.

In February 1915 the 13th Heavy Battery moved to Hampshire to complete their training.

On 30th May they were posted to France as part of the 17th Heavy Brigade.

After a few months on the Western Front, in October 1915, they joined the 28th Division to embark for Greece. The British Salonika Force was formed to deter Bulgaria from joining the Central Powers of Germany and Austria – Hungary in attacking neighbouring Serbia.

Jack travelled from Marseilles to Alexandria, Egypt, arriving on 22nd November, before moving on to Salonika on 4th January 1916.

The British Salonika Force along with French troops, planned to rush forward the 30 miles from Salonika to the Serbian border. They had to travel through mountain ranges which was very difficult as there were very few roads or bridges. They arrived too late as the Central Powers along with Bulgaria had invaded Serbia. The Serbians had fled, therefore there was no military need for British troops to stay in Salonika. However, it was considered that a British and French presence was necessary to save face after the failed Gallipoli campaign, therefore they were instructed to remain in Salonika.

It was very difficult for the troops on the Salonika Front as they found themselves a 'forgotten army' in a remote corner of Europe. The greatest killer was disease, especially malaria and dysentery.

Unfortunately, Jack was one of the many that contracted dysentery. He died on 10th December 1916, aged 24. He was buried at Salonika (Lembet Road) Military Cemetery in Thessaloniki, Greece. He is commemorated on the Welshpool War Memorial.

The Thomas family suffered more than most with the loss of two sons. Jack's younger brother, Edward, also fell in the Great War a short time later (story no. 18). They are both remembered on the family tombstone here at Christ Church.

'Gone but not forgotten'

13

George Henry Pryce

Lance Corporal :: Royal Welsh Fusiliers

Died :: 1st January 1917 :: At Sea

The memorial in the churchyard reads:

Lce. Corpl. George Henry Pryce

3rd Montgomeryshire Yeomanry

Beloved son of the above {Richard and Ann Pryce}

Who gave his life for his country on Jan 1 1917

Aged 21 years

Greater love hath no man than this, that he lay down his life for his friends.

"Come unto me, ye weary and I will give you rest."

George Henry Pryce was born in 1896 in Llandyssil, Montgomeryshire. He was the son of Richard and Annie Pryce, and he had two sisters, Emily and Florence. His father Richard originated from Leighton and his mother Annie from Berriew. When George was a young child, the family moved to Welshpool and ran The Raven Inn. As George grew up, he became involved in the family business and worked as a barman from at least the age of 15. His father Richard died in 1912, when George was 16, resulting in George helping his mother to run the inn and support the family.

The Raven Inn.

George enlisted in 1916, possibly staying home until then to support his family. On January 22nd 1916, George enlisted with the 3rd Battalion, Montgomeryshire Yeomanry. He was 20 years old. In May 1916 he was promoted to Lance Corporal.

On 20th December 1916 George embarked at Southampton to sail to Marseilles, France. On that same day he was transferred to the 15th Battalion Royal Welsh Fusiliers. At Marseilles, he boarded HT Ivernia. Along with 2400 other troops, they were bound for Alexandria, Egypt, sent as reinforcements.

S.S. Ivernia, Cunard Line.

The SS Ivernia was an ocean liner, owned by the Cunard Line. She was launched in 1899 and completed her maiden voyage from Liverpool to New York in April 1900. SS Ivernia was an 'immigration ship' carrying new settlers to America. At the outbreak of war in 1914, she was hired by the British Government to become a Troop Ship.

HT Ivernia left Marseilles on 28th December 1916 to sail across the Mediterranean to Alexandria, Egypt.

At 10:12am on 1st January 1917, the HT Ivernia was torpedoed by German Submarine UB-47. She was sailing in bad weather near Cape Matapan, Greece when she was struck. Approximately 120 people died, including George Pryce.

George is commemorated on the Mikra Memorial in Salonika (now known as Thessaloniki) in Greece.

George is also remembered on the Montgomeryshire Yeomanry memorial plaque inside St. Mary's Church, Welshpool, and on the Welshpool War Memorial.

'Greater love hath no man than this, that he lay down his life for his friends.'

14

Charles Trevor Bishop

Second Lieutenant :: 5th Batt. Wiltshire Regiment

Killed in Action :: 29th March 1917 :: Middle East

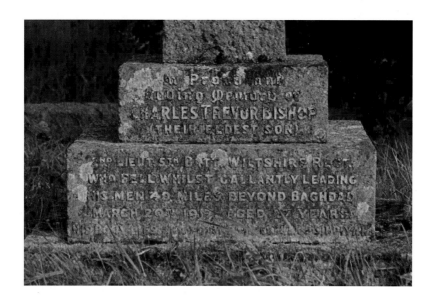

The memorial in the churchyard reads:

In proud and loving memory of

Charles Trevor Bishop (their {William & Margaret} eldest son)

2nd Lieut. 5th Batt. Wiltshire Regt.

Who fell whilst gallantly leading his men 40 miles beyond Baghdad

March 29th 1917   Aged 27 years

His body lies at a point 5 miles N.E. of Sindiyah

'Tranquil you lie, your knightly virtue proved. Your memory hallowed in the land you loved.'

Charles Trevor Bishop was born in Grantham, Lincolnshire in 1890. He was the son of William and Margaret Bishop. William originated from Upton Cressett in Shropshire and Margaret from Llanwrda, near Llandovery in Carmarthenshire. Charles was their eldest child, and he was later joined by a sister, Hilda, and a brother, William. Charles' father William was a chemist and ran his pharmacy business on Grantham's High Street. When Charles was a young child, the family moved to Welshpool and lived at 33 Broad Street, where William ran his Chemist's shop. The site is now part of the Premier shop and Post Office.

33 Broad Street.

Charles followed his father into the chemist's trade. In 1911, at the age of 21, he was working as a chemist's assistant in Blundellsands, near Liverpool.

With the outbreak of war in August 1914, Charles enrolled as 'ready for military service'. Utilising his skills in medicine, he was appointed to the 1st City of London Field Ambulance which was a Territorial Force of the Royal Army Medical Corps.

On 4th September 1914, the battalion embarked for Malta, arriving on 13th September. It is likely that he was involved in setting up hospitals on the island as in April 1915, Malta became the 'Nurse of the Mediterranean', receiving the sick and wounded from the Gallipoli campaign.

In June 1915, Charles was made Acting Sergeant. On 18th August 1915, Charles was given a commission with the 8th (Reserve) Battalion, Wiltshire Regiment. It is probable that he left Malta to return to the UK to train with his new regiment.

LIEUT. C. T. BISHOP.

Charles was made a Second Lieutenant and was transferred to the 5th Battalion, Wiltshire Regiment. He was posted to Mesopotamia, present day Iraq. He arrived in Bombay (now known as Mumbai) on 4th August 1916 before travelling on to Basra, arriving on 23rd September.

The focus of the British campaign in Mesopotamia was to protect the oil fields near Basra because the Royal Navy was heavily dependent on oil for its fleet of warships.

Mesopotamia was part of the Turkish Ottoman Empire, which was allied with Germany, therefore the British were keen to defeat the Turks. The Turkish Army was led by German 'advisors'.

In 1915 the British prepared to take the capital city of Baghdad. By 1916 British forces in the area were increasing along with additional troops from the Indian Army. They began to advance north up the River Tigris. Conditions were extremely difficult, and the Turks strongly resisted the British offensive.

With a change in British leadership of the campaign, they began to defeat the Turks and captured Baghdad on 11th March 1917. However, despite making significant advances in the area, no decisive victory was gained.

The war diaries of the Wiltshire Regiment states that they marched into Baghdad on the day that it fell into British hands. They were ordered to keep law and order as much looting had taken place. The inhabitants were very enthusiastic about their arrival and cheered the soldiers. From Baghdad, they marched north along the Tigris, clearing villages of snipers as they went. The villagers were very friendly and handed the men eggs and oranges as they passed.

On 29th March 1917, the 5th Wiltshire Regiment had reached Palm Tree Post and began to move forward along the Nahrwan Canal. As they advanced, they encountered heavy shell, machine gun and rifle fire, but they continued even though there was no cover. Casualties were high and Charles was killed. He was 27 years old. During the attack 28 men lost their lives and 141 were wounded. Brigadier General Lewin sent a message to the regiment saying, 'Well done Wilts, your advance was magnificent.'

By the following day, the Turks had evacuated their position.

Charles' body lies 5 miles northeast of Sindiyah.

Charles is commemorated on the Basra War Memorial in Iraq. He is also remembered on the Welshpool War Memorial.

In April 2015 Charles' war medals and Death Plaque were sold at an antiques auction in Oxfordshire.

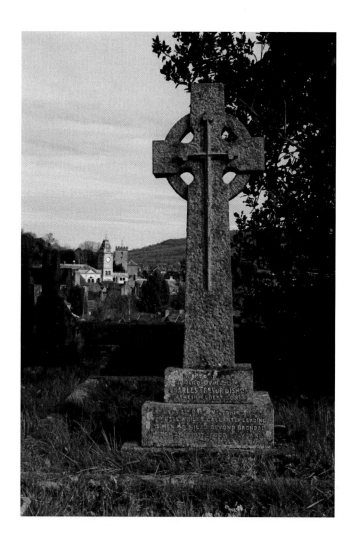

'Tranquil you lie, your knightly virtue proved.

Your memory hallowed in the land you loved.'

15

Harold Owen Davies

Private :: 54th Batt. Canadian Infantry

Killed in Action :: 9th April 2017 :: France & Flanders

The memorial in the churchyard reads:

Harold Owen Davies

Killed in action at Vimy Ridge

April 9th 1917

Aged 25 years

Harold Owen Davies was born on 29th January 1892 in Welshpool. He was the son of Edward and Mary Elizabeth Davies. Owen's father Edward originated from Berriew and was a mason. His mother Mary was from Liverpool. They lived in a large house called Bryneglwys on

Church Bank, opposite the junction with Red Bank. The house is no longer standing as it was demolished to enable the road to be widened.

The Davies family outside Bryneglwys. Owen is 2nd from left, back row.

The site of Bryneglwys.

Owen was one of 12 children, although his elder brother John died in infancy just days before Owen was born.

The family attended Welshpool Methodist Church.

In 1911, at the age of 19, Owen was working as a telegraph linesman, whilst still living at Bryneglwys. However, two years later, on 17th January 1913, Owen, along with his elder brother Trevor, emigrated to Canada. They sailed from Liverpool on the Hesperian to St John, New Brunswick.

Owen (left) with his elder brother Trevor. Canada, April 1913.

Owen and Trevor settled in Revelstoke in British Columbia. They both worked for the Canadian Pacific Railway, Owen as a linesman. Revelstoke was a major point on the transcontinental line, with divisional offices and depot situated there. Many employees of the

C.P.R. settled in the growing town. The area is very mountainous and today Revelstoke is a ski resort.

With the outbreak of war, Canada began a massive recruitment drive to send troops to Europe to assist the 'motherland'.

In June 1915, the 54th Kootney Battalion of the Canadian Infantry Regiment were mobilised at Vernon. The Battalion consisted of over 1000 men and had a black bear cub called Koots as its mascot. Along with many others from Revelstoke, both Owen and Trevor enlisted in the late summer of 1915 in Vernon.

After a few weeks, the third detachment of the 54th Kootney Battalion were sent to England. Owen and Trevor travelled across Canada to Halifax, Nova Scotia, which was a large Atlantic port. They boarded the transport liner Saxonia on 22nd November 1915.

Interestingly, the Saxonia was a sister ship to the Ivernia mentioned earlier in George Pryce's story (story no. 13) when she was torpedoed on New Year's Day 1917.

Built in 1899 as an Atlantic emigration liner, the Saxonia was used as a troop transport ship during the First World War. Unlike her sister ship, she survived the war and was finally scrapped in 1925.

Owen arrived in Plymouth on 2nd December 1915. The 54th Battalion were stationed at Bramshott Camp in Hampshire which was a temporary military camp set up by the Canadian Army.

In August 1916, the Battalion sailed to France, where it became part of the 4th Canadian Division, 11th Brigade. They were issued with steel helmets and gas masks and sent to Ypres on the Western Front to join the other Canadian Divisions. They were involved in several major battles during the Battle of the Somme.

During this time, Owen was awarded the Military Medal which is a recognition of gallantry and devotion to duty when under fire in battle on land.

In the Spring of 1917, the Canadian Army prepared to take Vimy Ridge, which was a 7km long ridge that gave the Germans a dominating view over Allied lines. Conditions were horrendous as the area was in effect an open graveyard as previous French attacks had failed with over 100,000 casualties.

The Canadian Army spent weeks planning the attack by using models and new maps and training their troops. Engineers dug deep tunnels to enable troops to get safely to the front. For the first time all four Canadian Divisions fought together in battle.

As one, the Canadian Army stormed the ridge at 5.30am on 9th April 1917. It was a cold Easter Monday, with sleet and snow. Over 15,000 Canadian Infantry attacked the Germans all along the front.

Canadian losses were huge that day. Owen was killed in action, along with over 100 of his comrades from the 54th Battalion. He was 25 years old.

After three more days of battle, the Canadian Army was victorious. It was an historic moment for the Canadian military. However, the cost was high with 3,598 Canadians killed and 7,000 wounded during the battle.

Owen was buried in the Canadian Cemetery No.2, Neuville-St. Vaast in France.

In Canada he is commemorated on the Revelstoke Cenotaph, and on a plaque outside the Revelstoke Courthouse. He is also listed on the Honour Rolls of both the Revelstoke Methodist Church and the YMCA.

In Welshpool, Owen is commemorated on the Welshpool War Memorial and on a brass plaque inside Welshpool Methodist Church.

War memorial plaque inside Welshpool Methodist Church.

A bronze 'Death Penny' was given to the next of kin of each of the fallen during the First World War. Owen's has been mounted on the family headstone.

Owen Davies' memorial plaque.

Further tragedy was to befall the Davies family shortly after Owen's death as another son, James Wilfred Davies, was to fall on the battlefields of France and Flanders (story no. 17), hence why there are two Death Pennies mounted on the family headstone.

Owen's brother Trevor survived the war and returned to Canada. He had served as a medic in the same unit as Owen. In May 1917, he was sent to Buxton in Derbyshire to convalesce from trench fever, where he met his wife, Freda. When he had recovered and the war was over, Trevor returned to Revelstoke and resumed working for the Canadian Pacific Railway. He was soon joined by Freda, and they settled in Winnipeg, where they brought up their family.

16

Charles Herbert Morris

Lieutenant :: 13th Batt. Royal Welsh Fusiliers attached to 59th Royal Flying Corps

Missing in Action :: 13th April 1917 :: France & Flanders

The memorial in the churchyard reads:

Also of

Lieut. Charles Herbert Morris

13th RWF attached to 59th RAF

Born Feb 4th 1892

Missing in France April 13th 1917

Charles Herbert Morris was born on 4th February 1892 in Welshpool. He was the son of William and Jane Morris. They had 17 children, although one died in infancy, and Charles was their youngest son. His elder brother was Edwin Morris who also served and died in the First World War (story no. 10).

William originated from Berriew and he was a draper by trade. He ran his business from 4 High Street (where Costa's is today). Jane originated from Burgh-Le-Marsh in Lincolnshire. The family lived at Severn Villa, which was located near the canal, now part of Little Henfaes Lane. The building is no longer standing, but there is evidence of the former residence with a gateway in the stone wall alongside the canal.

Evidence of a former entrance to Severn Villa.

Charles attended Lampeter College School. He continued his education by entering St. David's College, Lampeter in October 1912, with the intention of taking Holy Orders.

As well as being very academic, Charles was an accomplished sportsman. He played for the college rugby, hockey and football teams and achieved athletic success in the College Sports.

At the outbreak of war, Charles enlisted with the Royal Welsh Fusiliers, 13th (Service) Battalion and was given a commission as Lieutenant. The 13th Battalion was raised in Rhyl in September 1914. In December he went to France and joined one of the regular battalions on the battlefield. In 1916 he fought in the Battle for Mametz Wood, on the Somme.

Lieutenant Charles Herbert Morris.

In the summer of 1916, Charles was attached to the Royal Flying Corps (which later became the RAF) as an observer. He was posted to 59 Squadron, a reconnaissance squadron which formed at Narborough Airfield, Norfolk on 1st August 1916. The Squadron was deployed to Saint-Omer in northern France on 13th February 1917. They were equipped with Royal Aircraft Factory RE8 planes, which were fitted with cameras to photograph enemy targets.

Charles was involved in photo reconnaissance and spotting work for the Royal Artillery during the Battle of Arras.

On the morning of Friday 13th April 1917, Charles took off aboard RE8, Serial A3416. He was an observer with Captain George Bailey Hodgson, and they were under orders to photograph targets around Etaing, near Arras. Their plane was shot down, along with five others from the squadron, by a group of six technologically superior German Albatros Scouts led by Rittmeister Manfred von Richthofen, 'The Red Baron'. It is recorded that 'machine did not return owing to casualty'. Their bodies were never found. It was at the height of what the Royal Flying

Corps refer to as 'Bloody April' as losses were so high and life expectancy was just 23 days.

Charles was 25 years old.

Charles is commemorated on the Arras Flying Services Memorial in France. He is also commemorated on several other war memorials including in St. David's College, Lampeter; in Rhyl (possibly because the 13th Battalion of the Royal Welsh Fusiliers were raised there. The Roll of Honour mentions a Mrs F. J. Gamlin, who was Charles' sister and lived in Rhyl) and on the Welshpool War Memorial.

Inside Christ Church, adjacent to the south door is a bronze plaque erected by Charles' mother and siblings, which commemorates both Charles and his brother Edwin. Their cousin Richard also fell in the Great War (story no. 20).

Bronze memorial plaque situated inside Christ Church.

The Morris family plot.

17

James Wilfred Davies

Private :: Machine Gun Corps

Killed in Action :: 24th April 1917 :: France & Flanders

The memorial in the churchyard reads:

James Wilfred Davies

Killed in action near Arras

April 24th 1917   Aged 22 years

James Wilfred Davies was born in 1895 in Welshpool and was the son of Edward and Mary Elizabeth Davies. He was a younger brother to Harold Owen Davies (story no. 15). Wilfred's father Edward was a mason by trade. The family lived at Bryneglwys on Church Street in Welshpool. Bryneglwys has since been demolished to widen the road on the corner of Church Bank.

Wilfred, centre, outside Bryneglwys.

Site of Bryneglwys.

In 1911, at the age of 16, Wilfred left Welshpool to live near Bilston (now part of Wolverhampton). He was staying with his second cousin's family at Batman's Hill House and working as a joiner's apprentice.

With the outbreak of war, Wilfred enlisted and became a Private with the Machine Gun Corps. Most of the records for the Machine Gun Corps were destroyed in a fire, therefore it is not known exactly when Wilfred enlisted. The Machine Gun Corps was formed in October 1915 when it became clear that for the British Army to be an effective force on the Western Front there needed to be a dedicated and specially trained unit of machine gunners. A depot and training centre was established at Belton Park in Grantham, Lincolnshire. Belton Park was a large private estate and mansion house owned by the Earl and Countess Brownlow. At the outbreak of war in 1914, they donated the use of the parkland to the War Office. In 1915 it became the base for the newly formed Machine Gun Corps. The camp consisted of wooden huts, a military hospital, churches, YMCA huts and a railway line; all of which remained until 1920.

It was a requirement that men had to be in good physical condition to be admitted to the Machine Gun Corps as they had to be able to carry heavy equipment. They also needed to be intelligent and technically minded to operate, maintain and repair their Vickers machine gun. Machine Gunners also needed the ability to respond to orders quickly, communicate well in difficult conditions, map read and signal. As a front-line force, the men of the Machine Gun Corps were often involved in brave and heroic situations. However, casualties were high, giving it the nickname 'the Suicide Club'.

After training at Belton Park, Wilfred became part of the 51st Company, Machine Gun Corps. In February 1916 they sailed to France and joined the 17th Division. As a unit of the 17th Division, they were likely to have been involved in The Battles of the Somme and the Battles of Arras. The Battles of Arras started well for the Allies, with more ground taken at Vimy Ridge and the First Battle of the Scarpe since trench warfare began. Encouraged, they paused to allow for a rotation of exhausted troops before starting on the third phase of the attack. The Second Battle of the Scarpe took place on 23rd – 24th April 1917.

Wilfred was killed in action on 24th April 1917, just 15 days after his brother Owen had died a few miles away. He was 22 years old.

Wilfred's body was never found. He is commemorated on the Arras Memorial in France.

Wilfred is also commemorated on a brass plaque in the Welshpool Methodist Church and on the Welshpool War Memorial.

To THE GLORY OF GOD
AND IN SACRED MEMORY OF
HAROLD OWEN DAVIES
JAMES WILFRED DAVIES
GEORGE EVANS
THOMAS LEONARD EVANS
JAMES WILLIAM JOHNSON
WILLIAM MERCER
WILLIAM WILKINSON

WHO GAVE THEIR LIVES IN THE GREAT WAR
1914—1919
"FAITHFUL UNTO DEATH"

Brass memorial inside Welshpool Methodist Church.

Wilfred's bronze Death Penny has been mounted on the headstone of the family grave in Christ Church churchyard, alongside his brother Owen's.

Wilfred Davies' bronze Death Penny.

Interestingly, another brother George became a missionary in South Africa. He returned to Welshpool in the 1930's and was an active member of a pre-war peace group.

18

Edward Thomas

Private :: Cheshire Regiment

Killed in Action :: 22nd October 2017 :: France & Flanders

The memorial in the churchyard reads:

And of their {William & Elizabeth} sons,

John and Edward,

Who fell in the Great War.

R. I. P.

Edward 'Ned' Thomas was born in 1896 in Welshpool. He was the youngest son of William and Elizabeth Thomas, and brother to John 'Jack' Thomas (story no. 12). His father William was a labourer and the family lived at 47 Lledan Crescent. The house is no longer standing as the crescent was demolished and is now the site of the former Welshpool Library.

Lledan Crescent past and present.

Ned was 17 years old when war broke out. He enlisted with the Royal Welsh Fusiliers, and was later transferred to the 16th Battalion, Cheshire Regiment. Due to heavy losses on the Western Front in 1916, the Battalion received new men transferred from disbanded yeomanry regiments. Ned may have been transferred to the Battalion at this time.

Edward Thomas, left, and his elder brother John.

In 1917, the 16th Battalion were in France and Flanders on the Western Front. They took part in the Battle of Passchendaele in an attempt to control the ridges near Ypres, a Belgium city. The weather was very wet in October 1917 and the battlefields had become a quagmire. After several days of fair weather, on 22nd October, the 16th Battalion as part of the 35th Division, attacked northwards into Houthulst Forest. They were supported by a regiment of the French 1st Division on the left flank. The ground was still soaked and cut up by bombardments and they struggled to advance. The German Army defended well and were able to counterattack, consequently pushing the Division back.

Ned was killed in action on 22nd October 1917. He was 21 years old. He has no known grave. He is commemorated on the Tyne Cot Memorial to the Missing near Ypres, Belgium. He is also commemorated on the Welshpool War Memorial.

Edward's elder brother John also died in the First World War (story no. 12). Edward and John are the third set of brothers to fall in the Great War that are remembered here at Christ Church.

R. I. P.

19

Richard William Harold Thomas

Trooper :: Household Battalion

Died of Wounds :: 10th December 1917 :: France & Flanders

The memorial in the churchyard reads:

Also of Trooper R. W. H. Thomas,

Son of the above {William & Naomi Thomas},

Died of wounds (interred Tilloy France)

Dec. 10th 1917, Aged 27 years.

Richard William Harold Thomas was born in Welshpool in 1891. He was the eldest son of William and Naomi Thomas. His father William originated from Welshpool and was a cabinet maker by trade. His mother Naomi was from Priest Weston. The family lived at 24 Raven Street. The house has since been demolished and new bungalows have been built on the site. In later years the family lived at 6 Raven Street.

Raven Street.

The 1901 census shows that Harold, aged 10, was staying with his mother's family near Churchstoke.

At the age of 20, in 1911, Harold was working as a baker in Weston Rhyn near Gobowen, Oswestry.

With the outbreak of war, Harold enlisted with the Household Battalion, possibly in January 1917. He may have served in a different regiment beforehand as the Household Battalion was formed from troops of the Household Cavalry. More infantrymen were needed on the Western Front, so the cavalrymen were retrained as foot soldiers.

During 1917, the Household Battalion were involved in the Battle of the Somme, the Battle of Arras, the Third Battle of Ypres (Passchendaele) and the Battle of Cambrai in late November/early December.

Harold died from wounds on 10th December 1917. He is buried at Tilloy British Cemetery, Tilloy-Les-Mofflaines near Arras, France. He was 27 years old.

Harold is commemorated on the Welshpool War Memorial.

'Safe in the arms of Jesus.'

20

Richard Lewis Morris

Private :: Border Regiment

Killed in Action :: 13th April 1918 :: France & Flanders

The memorial in the churchyard reads:

In loving memory of Richard Lewis Morris

Who was killed in France,

April 1918.

Richard Lewis Morris was born in 1880 in Welshpool. He was the son of Morgan and Mary Morris and was their sixth child. Morgan originated from Berriew and Mary was from Guilsfield. The family lived in Gungrog Lane, before residing in Trefalgar House (now known as Hen Blas) on Salop Road.

Hen Blas, Salop Road.

Richard's father Morgan ran The Foundry with his brother John. J. & M. Morris Ltd was an iron and brass foundry, and a significant business in Welshpool. There are many references to their trade still visible around the town. The Morris brothers were very influential businessmen. Another of Morgan's brothers, William Morris, was a draper and flannel mill owner, and was the father to Edwin and Charles Morris who also fell in the Great War (stories no. 10 and 16 respectfully).

J. & M. Morris manhole cover; many are still visible within the Welshpool area.

J. & M. Morris gas lamp post in Christ Church churchyard.

Evidence of the site of the Foundry.

J. & M. Morris Agricultural Depot.

As a young man Richard lived in Bootle, Lancashire, working as a grocer's assistant. He lived in Bootle for over 10 years and boarded with Alice Parkes and her aunt at a house first on Strand Road, then on nearby Bank Road. He continued to work as a grocer's assistant throughout that time.

After war broke out, Richard enlisted with the 1st Battalion, Border Regiment in Seaforth, Lancashire. It is not known when Richard enlisted or exactly what military action he was involved in, but the Border Regiment saw significant action during the First World War. They went to Gallipolli in 1915 and after being evacuated to Egypt in January 1916, were posted to France where they were involved in the Battle of the Somme. During 1917, the battalion saw action in the Arras

Offensive (the 1st, 2nd and 3rd Battles of the Scarpe). They were then moved to the battlefields of Flanders. In April 1918, as part of the 29th Division, the battalion fought in the Battle of Hazebrouck, which was part of the Battle of Lys. Included in this battle was the Defence of Nieppe Forest which saw the 29th and 31st Divisions defend a line east against overwhelming forces. The German Army's objective was to capture key railway and supply roads to cut off the British Second Army at Ypres. Initially they had some success, but the British and French armies held firm.

Richard was killed in action on 13th April 1918. He was 38 years old. His body was never found. He is commemorated on the Ploegsteert Memorial, Hainaut, Belguim, a memorial to the Missing with no known grave.

Richard is also commemorated on the Welshpool War Memorial.

R. I. P.

21

William Longhurst

Private :: Royal Welsh Fusiliers

Killed in Action :: 22nd April 1918 :: France & Flanders

The memorial to William is in the form of the bronze plaque that was issued to the next of kin of those that fell in the Great War which is mounted (top right) on his wife's headstone in the churchyard.

William Longhurst was born in 1882 in Banbury, Oxfordshre. He was the son of George William and Elizabeth Longhurst. His father originated from Bodicote near Banbury and was a brewer's clerk by profession. He died when William was a young child. Elizabeth originated from Llanymynech and possibly moved back to her home area after the death of her husband, as in 1891 the family were living at The Farm in Llanymynech. William's military records wrongly state that he was born in Llanymynech. It seems likely from the census of 1901 that he worked as a domestic groom in Llansaintfraidd-ym-Mechain when he was a young man of 18. However, the census states that he was born in Marton, Shropshire, so it may well be a different William. The 1911 census lists a George William Longhurst boarding at 10 Lledan Terrace, Brook Street, Welshpool. He was 28, single and working as a grocer. It was noted that he had a dray – a cart without sides used for delivering heavy loads.

10 Lledan Terrace, Brook Street.

It could have been around this time that William enlisted with the Montgomeryshire Yeomanry, the local militia.

Just after war broke out in September 1914, the Royal Welsh Fusiliers were raised and joined the Division at Llandudno. It is likely that William was among them as he was drafted into the 13th Battalion, Royal Welsh Fusiliers.

Just before the Battalion moved to Winchester for their final training, on 9th July 1915, William married Mary Harriet Jones at St. Mary's

Parish Church in Welshpool. He resided at Greenwood Villa, Mill Lane and his profession was recorded as 'Soldier'. Mary was a sister to Herbert Jones who also died in the First World War a short time after William's death (story no. 27).

Greenwood Villa, Mill Lane.

In August 1915 the 13th Battalion of the Royal Welsh Fusiliers went to Winchester to complete their training before embarking to France in December 1915.

In July 1916, as part of the 38th Division, they saw action at Mametz Wood on the Somme and suffered heavy losses. In 1917, they saw action again in the Third Battles of Ypres. They returned to the Somme in 1918 and fought in the Battles of the Hindenburg Line.

William was killed in action on 22nd April 1918 near the village of Bouzincourt. The village was on the Somme and had been in German occupation until March 1918.

William was 35 years old.

In September 1918, the first area of the Bouzincourt Ridge Cemetery was formed by the V. Corps Burial Officer who cleared the battlefields. After the Armistice 500 graves were brought in from the immediate area. This was part of the 'concentration of graves', which exhumed those in smaller or isolated cemeteries and reburied them in an established military cemetery to ensure proper commemoration by the Commonwealth War Graves Commission.

William's body was exhumed and reburied in the Bouzincourt Ridge Cemetery in April 1920.

William is commemorated on the Welshpool War Memorial.

William's 'Death Penny', the bronze plaque issued to the next of kin of all those who fell in the Great War, is mounted on Mary's headstone. She died in 1936 and is buried with her parents and other family members. The headstone includes a memorial to her brother Herbert who also fell in the Great War a short time after William (story no. 27). His Death Penny is also mounted on the headstone.

Bronze 'Death Penny' memorial to William Longhurst.

'Peace perfect peace'

22

Thomas Leonard Jones

Private :: South Wales Borderers

Died of Wounds :: 30th April 1918 :: Germany

The memorial in the churchyard reads:

In loving memory of Thomas Leonard Jones

Who died of wounds received in action April 30th 1918

Aged 42 years

Interred in South Cemetery, Cologne

'In hope of a joyful resurrection.'

Thomas Leonard Jones was born in Welshpool in 1876. He was the son of Thomas Samuel and Margaret Jones and the youngest of their three children. His father was a mason and his mother, who originated from Trelystan, was a dressmaker. The family lived in Brook Cottage, Raven Square, which was next door to The Raven Inn (where George Pryce (story no. 13) lived).

Brook Cottage, Raven Square.

Brook Cottage, Raven Square.

Leonard's father died when he was a young boy. In 1891, at aged 15, Leonard was working as a grocer's apprentice.

By 1908 the family were living at 12 Mount Street.

The family had more difficult times to endure when Leonard's sister Lucy died in 1908, followed by his eldest sister Margaret in 1909.

Leonard continued to live with his mother at 12 Mount Street, working as a grocer.

12 Mount Street.

On 8th August 1912, at the age of 36, Leonard married Elizabeth Charlotte Smith at St. Mary's Parish Church, Welshpool.

With the outbreak of war, Leonard enlisted with the 2nd Battalion of the South Wales Borderers in Newport, Monmouthshire (now Gwent). It is not known exactly when he enlisted, and his military history is unknown. The Battalion served in the Gallipoli campaign in 1915, and during 1916 and 1917 they saw action in France and Flanders with the Third Battle of Ypres and at Cambrai. In April 1918 the Battalion were involved in combating the German offensive on the Lys.

On 11th April, Leonard was reported missing whilst in action on the front line at Estaires. Leonard had sustained injuries to his right knee and left upper thigh. He was captured by the German Army and became a Prisoner of War. He was sent to Limburg, a holding camp where he received medical attention before moving to a camp in Cologne which had hospitals treating British Prisoners of War. However, Leonard died due to the wounds he had received on 30th April 1918.

He was 42 years old.

Leonard was buried at South Cemetery in Cologne.

He is commemorated on the Welshpool War Memorial.

'In hope of a joyful resurrection'

23

John Henry Owen

Private :: Royal Welsh Fusiliers

Missing in Action :: 14th June 1918 :: France & Flanders

The memorial in the churchyard reads:

Also of John Henry, their {James and Sarah} son.

Killed on active service 14th June 1918

Aged 34 years.

John Henry Owen was born in 1884 and was the son of James Colley and Sarah Owen. His mother Sarah originated from Great Ness in Shropshire. The family lived and farmed at Trefnant Fechan near Cloddiau but later moved to Groespluen Farm, just outside Welshpool.

John was one of four boys. His eldest brother Alfred later emigrated to Canada. John and his brother James worked on the farm as young boys. John's father died in 1912, leaving the two brothers to run the farm with their mother.

Groespluen Farm.

On 12th December 1915, at the age of 30, John enlisted with the 1/4th Battalion, Royal Welsh Fusiliers. His brother and mother continued to run the farm.

The 1/4th (Denbighshire) Battalion was part of the Territorial Force. It is not known exactly what military action John was involved in, but at the end of March 1918 John was transferred to the 9th Battalion as a Private. The Battalion saw action on the Somme. The Battle of Aisne began on 27th May 1918.

The following day, during the battle, John was reported missing, presumably killed in action. His body was never found and on 14th June his 'death was accepted for official purposes'.

John is commemorated on the Soissons Memorial in Aisne, France which commemorates almost 4000 British men who died in the Battles of the Aisne and the Marne in 1918 who have no known grave.

John is also commemorated on both the Welshpool War Memorial and Guilsfield War Memorial.

Guilsfield War Memorial.

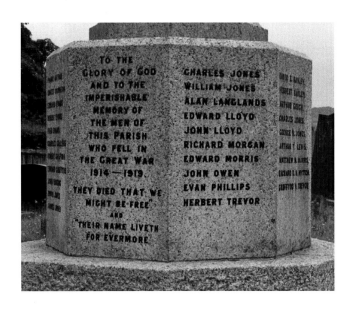

The Owen family plot.

24

Reginald Valentine Manford

Lieutenant :: Royal Field Artillery

Killed in Action :: 8th August 1918 :: France & Flanders

The memorial in the churchyard reads:

Also of Rex, son of Samuel and Edith Manford

Lieutenant R.F.A.

Killed in action in France

8th August 1918.

Aged 26 years.

Reginald 'Rex' Valentine Manford was born in Welshpool in 1892. He was the son of Samuel and Edith Manford. His father Samuel originated from Melverley near Oswestry and his mother Edith from Kinnerley, also near Oswestry. Rex had an elder brother, Ronald, and a younger sister, Edith. His father Samuel worked for the Earl of Powis as the Estate Cashier.

Rex was baptised at Christ Church on 20th March 1892.

The family lived at 17 High Street (now the offices of an accountancy firm). By 1911, the family had moved to Stone House.

17 High Street.

Sometime later the family moved to Springbank, a cottage just outside of Welshpool on the Llanfair Caereinion road.

A view of Springbank cottage.

Rex was educated at the Grammar School in Welshpool, and he won many school prizes during his time there. Both he and his brother Ronald were members of the Christ Church choir. In later years Rex was the organist for Forden Church and would frequently play the organ here at Christ Church.

Christ Church choir, 1905.

Rex Manford as a young choir boy.

At the age of 19, Rex was working alongside his father and brother for the Earl of Powis as an Estate Clerk. He later became the Earl of Powis' Private Secretary.

Several months before war broke out, on 2nd March 1914, Rex enlisted with the Montgomeryshire Yeomanry. On 21st May 1914, he was promoted to Lance-Corporal Artificer in the Motorcycle Section. A short time later he became a Sergeant. His Army training was conducted in Welshpool and Bedford.

On 22nd February 1915 Rex received a commission as Lieutenant with the Royal Field Artillery (Chester Brigade).

The Royal Field Artillery were responsible for the medium calibre guns and howitzers. They had to work close to the front line. The 'trench mortar' was a new form of artillery which was developed for the Western Front. Whilst the lighter weapons were carried by the Infantry, the Royal Field Artillery manned the heavier mortars.

On 21st November 1915, Rex arrived in France and Flanders and was involved in battles on the Western Front. Rex was posted to Egypt in February 1916. Whilst there he was wounded in the knee during the winter of 1917. Rex was in one of the first batteries to enter Jerusalem in December 1917.

In June 1918, Rex volunteered to be drafted to the Western Front.

Six weeks later, on 8th August 1918, Rex was killed in action whilst serving as a Lieutenant with the 59th Battery Royal Field Artillery in the 18th Army Brigade. He died at Treux, in the region of the Somme. He was 26 years old.

Rex is buried in the Ribemont Communal Cemetery Extention, Somme.

Ribemont Communal Cemetery Extension.

Rex Manford's headstone.

Rex is commemorated on a brass plaque inside Christ Church. It is situated on the north wall of the church.

Brass plaque inside Christ Church.

The plaque was made by F. Osborne and Co. Ltd., and the engraver was Sidney Hunt. They were based in London and began as engravers before specialising in war memorial plaques, ecclesiastical silver and other church metal work.

Rex is also commemorated on the Welshpool War Memorial.

Rex's 'Death Penny' has been incorporated into the family headstone.

Rex Manford's 'Death Penny'.

In 2008 his war medals were sold at auction in London for £120.

'Till the barrage lifts'

25

William Herbert Waring

Sergeant :: Royal Welsh Fusiliers

Died of Wounds :: 8th October 1918 :: France & Flanders

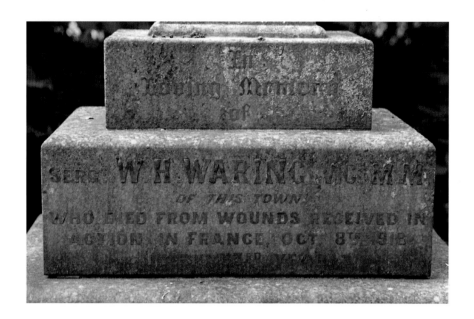

The memorial in the churchyard reads:

In loving memory of

Sergt. W. H. Waring V.C. M.M.

Of this town

Who died from wounds received in action in France.

Oct. 8th 1918 in his 33rd year.

William Herbert Waring was born on 13th October 1885 in Welshpool. He was the third son to Richard and Annie Elizabeth Waring, who both originated from Welshpool. They had ten children but lost four during infancy. The family lived in Raven Street before moving to Rock Terrace in Raven Square. William's father Richard was a nail maker and later became a fishmonger.

Raven Square.

As a child, William attended Christ Church Infants School and the Boys National School in Berriew Road.

Christ Church Infant School, now Kingswood.

In 1901, as a young man of 18, William was working as a labourer on the Elan Valley Reservoir Scheme and living in the Elan Village near Rhayader. In 1904 he returned to Welshpool and worked as a feather-er for a local poultry dealer.

William was a keen sportsman and particularly enjoyed playing football. He was a member of the local teams.

It is likely that William attended Christ Church and was possibly a choir boy here as there is a signature of a 'W Waring' in pencil on a wooden door inside the back of the church, which the choir boys would have had access to.

Inscription on a door inside Christ Church.

William joined the Montgomeryshire Yeomanry in 1904. He attended many training camps; some of which took place in Maesgwasted field behind Christ Church. William thrived in the Army and was promoted to Corporal in 1911 and Sergeant in 1913.

Before war broke out, William was working as a butcher.

The Montgomeryshire Yeomanry was embodied at the outbreak of war in August 1914. William was put in charge of getting horses for the regiment. The Yeomanry were sent to Norfolk to train and defend the coast.

On 3rd March 1916, the regiment was posted to Egypt. They sailed from Devonport to Alexandria, arriving on 13th March. During the voyage the transport ship narrowly avoided two U-Boat attacks.

The regiment had another period of training and reorganisation. On New Year's Day in 1917 they became part of the newly formed 25th Royal Welsh Fusiliers.

In April 1917 the Regiment moved to the front line near Gaza as pioneers which involved digging trenches and putting up fences. In November they attacked Turkish positions. During this action William was awarded the Military Medal for showing great courage.

Sergeant William Waring.

In April 1918 William's regiment left Egypt and sailed to Marseilles, arriving on 7th May. William had four days leave at home before being drafted to the Western Front where he fought at the Somme in the final push to defeat the German Armies.

On 18th September 1918 William was wounded in battle.

The official account of William's final actions was published in the London Gazette on 31st January 1919 and is as follows:

'SERGEANT WILLIAM WARING, M.M., 1/1 Montgomery Yeomanry and 25th Royal Welsh Fusiliers.

For most conspicuous bravery and devotion to duty at Ronssoy on 18th September 1918. He led an attack against enemy machine guns which were holding up the advance of neighbouring troops and in the face of devastating fire from flank and front, single handed, rushed a strong point, bayonetting four of the garrison and capturing two with their guns. Sergt. Waring then under heavy shell and machine gun fire, reorganised his men and led and inspired them for another 400 yards, when he fell mortally wounded. His valour, determination and leadership were conspicuous throughout.'

William was evacuated by Field Ambulance and taken to the General Hospital at La Havre. He died on 8th October 1918 just days before his 33rd birthday.

William is buried at Ste Marie Cemetery, La Havre, France.

For his valour in battle, William was awarded the Victoria Cross posthumously. The Victoria Cross is one of the highest military decorations which was awarded for valour in the face of the enemy. King George V presented the VC medal to William's father Richard on 8th March 1919 at Buckingham Palace.

The Waring family leaving Buckingham Palace.

William's mother Annie donated William's VC medal to Montgomeryshire Borough Council in 1929, as she felt that she couldn't leave it to just one of her two surviving sons. It is held in a bank vault, with a replica medal on display in the Town Hall, Welshpool.

William is commemorated on the Welshpool War Memorial and on the Montgomeryshire Yeomanry plaque inside St. Mary's Church, Welshpool.

Montgomeryshire Yeomanry Plaque, St. Mary's Church.

Montgomeryshire Yeomanry plaque, St. Mary's Church.

In 2015 as part of a UK Government First World War Centenary campaign, a commemorative paving stone was unveiled on the wall of the Town Hall. The paving stones were issued to be laid at the birth places of VC recipients of the First World War.

LANCE SERGEANT
WILLIAM WARING
THE ROYAL WELSH FUSILIERS
18TH SEPTEMBER 1918

BORN: Oct 13 1888
DIED: Oct 8 1918

WORLD WAR 1 VICTORIA CROSS RECIPIENT
BORN IN WELSHPOOL, MONTGOMERYSHIRE, MID WALES
HE SERVED AS A SERGEANT IN THE 25TH BATTALION
ROYAL WELSH FUSILIERS, BRITISH ARMY

Commemorative paving stone outside Welshpool Town Hall.

'In our hearts he still lives'

26

Harry Rudge

New Zealand Reserves

Died :: 22nd November 1918 :: New Zealand

The memorial in the churchyard reads:

In loving memory of

Harry Rudge

Died in New Zealand from effects of war service,

Nov. 22nd 1918.   Aged 26 Years.

The story of Harry Rudge has been one of the hardest to trace and consequentially there are some puzzling gaps.

Harry was born in Welshpool in 1891 and was the fourth child to William Harry and Jane Elizabeth Rudge. The family owned the

Mermaid Inn in Welshpool. His father William originated from Shifnal, Shropshire and his mother Jane from Castle Caereinion.

The Mermaid Inn.

Harry's father William was an accomplished horse rider and sportsman. Whilst training, a horse took fright and kicked William's head resulting in his death on 6th July 1896. Harry's mother continued to run the Mermaid Inn.

Harry doesn't appear locally on the census until 1911 at the age of 19, even though the family had been living at the Mermaid Inn for over 20 years before that. In 1901, at aged 10, Harry was living as a boarder in Halton (now part of Runcorn) in Cheshire. Another boarder in the house was Alice M. Evans, a 23-year-old schoolteacher who was born in Welshpool. It is not known why Harry was living in Cheshire.

For some time during this research, it was presumed that Harry was the preferred name of his brother Albert Henry since Harry was absent from any found records during his childhood. However, it later transpired that Albert Henry was in fact Harry's brother. He became the Landlord of the Bridge Inn in Chirk and died in 1953, aged 68. Interestingly Harry's other brother Hubert (Herbert) also followed the family trade by becoming the Landlord of the Eagles Inn in Llanfyllin. Sadly, similarly to his father, he died in a horse-riding accident at a young age.

By 1911 Harry had returned to Welshpool, living at the Mermaid Inn with his mother Jane. He was 19 years old and working as a 'dealer in skins'. He was also a keen sportsman.

At some point during 1913, Harry emigrated to New Zealand. He declared his occupation as a butcher. In September 1914 Harry became engaged to Gladys Baldwin and they married a short time later. Harry and Gladys settled in Wellington where Harry worked as a labourer and driver. In 1916 they had a daughter, Dorothy Gladys.

Harry does not appear on any military war records in New Zealand, therefore it is not clear what Harry's war service, if any, was. The only reference found is that Harry was on the New Zealand Reserves lists during the war years.

In 1918 New Zealand was hit by the devastating Great Influenza epidemic and Harry was one of its casualties. He died in the Wellington College Temporary Hospital of Influenza. Harry was buried in Wellington and his headstone reads:

In fond memory of

Harry, husband of Gladys Rudge

2nd December 1918

28 Years

'If love could have saved him he never would have died.'

There is a discrepancy in the date of death and his age. On the gravestone here at Christ Church it states that he died on 22nd November 1918 and that he was 26 years old (although the baptism record would age Harry at 27 when he died). The gravestone also states that he died from the 'effects of war service'. Perhaps with the distances involved there were some communication errors.

There remains a lot more to research with this story and hopefully more information will come to light in the future.

'If love could have saved him he never would have died'

27

Herbert Jones

Private :: Royal Air Force

Died :: 11th December 1918 :: UK

The memorial in the churchyard reads:

In loving memory of

Herbert Jones

1885 – 1918

Herbert Jones was born in Welshpool on 7th February 1885 and was the fifth child to William and Elizabeth Jones. His father William originated from Welshpool and was a domestic gardener by trade. His mother Elizabeth originated from Llanidloes. The family lived at 49 Mount Street. When Herbert was a young boy, his father died.

49 Mount Street.

In 1901, at aged 16, Herbert was working as an 'aerated water bottle washer'. Ten years later he was working as a postman while still living in the family home.

Shortly after the outbreak of war, Herbert enlisted as a labourer possibly with the Royal Flying Corps (which later became the Royal Air Force). He became an aircraft hand in May 1917. It is not known where he was based.

In October 1917 Herbert married Rose Smith, whose father was Head Carpenter at Powis Castle.

Towards the end of 1918, Herbert was admitted to Connaught Hospital in Farnborough, Hampshire, suffering with influenza and pneumonia. He died on 11th December 1918 and is buried here at Christ Church.

Rose went on to live at Oldford Cottage. On her death she was buried with Herbert here at Christ Church.

Oldford Cottage.

Herbert's bronze 'Death Penny' is mounted on the headstone, along with his brother-in-law's William Longhurst (story no. 21).

Herbert Jones' bronze 'Death Penny'.

Herbert is commemorated on the Welshpool War Memorial.

'Peace perfect peace'

28

John Rimmer

Private :: Labour Corps

Died :: 14th November 1919 :: UK

The memorial in the churchyard reads:

419553 Private J Rimmer

Labour Corps

14th November 1919

Age 27

Peace perfect peace

John Rimmer was born in 1890 in Chirbury, Shropshire. He was the sixth child of John and Jane Rimmer. His father John, a gamekeeper by profession, originated from Denbighshire and his mother Jane from Chester. The family lived at Upper Park Cottage in Stockton near Forden, later living at Stockton Wood.

In 1911, at aged 22, John was living at The Moat, Welshpool and working as a 'waggoner on farm' for Richard Davies. The Moat farm is just outside Welshpool on the Newtown Road.

John married Mary and they had a daughter, Catherine Mabel. They lived at 6 Powell's Lane, Off High Street, Welshpool. Later Mary lived further up the road at 7 Mount Pleasant.

Powell's Lane.

Mount Pleasant.

With the outbreak of war, John enlisted with the Lancashire Fusiliers, 2nd Battalion in April 1915.

On 4th April 1916, he embarked the HT Aragon to be transported to Egypt and arrived on 23rd April. John served in Egypt until 23rd February 1917 when he was posted to France.

Whilst fighting on the battlefields in France, he suffered a shrapnel wound to his left eye. After treatment in hospital, he returned to serve in the trenches of the Western Front.

In September 1918 John returned to Britain and was posted to the Agricultural Distribution Centre at Wrexham, possibly because of the long-term effects of his wounds. He had completely lost the sight in his left eye and his right eye was worsening.

John was discharged from the Labour Corps on 7th March 1919 'being surplus to military requirements'. It was noted that he had 'suffered impairments since entry into the service'.

John died on 14th November 1919. It is not known at present what caused his death and whether it was due to his wounds. He is buried here at Christ Church.

'Peace perfect peace'

29

Cyril Patrick Pryce Yearsley

Montgomeryshire Yeomanry

Died :: 8th January 1920 :: UK

The memorial in the churchyard reads:

Also Cyril Patrick Pryce, their son {Charles and Lizzie Elenor}

Who died January 8th 1920

Aged 19 years.

'Abide with me.'

Cyril Patrick Pryce Yearsley was born in 1900 in Welshpool. He was baptised on 11th April 1900. He was the son of Charles and Lizzie Elenor Pryce Yearsley and was the youngest of their three children. His father Charles was a solicitor and a partner with Gilbert Davies Solicitors, Severn Street.

The family lived at 25 Severn Street (where Cadwalader's Accountants is today).

25 Severn Street.

By 1911 the family were living at Bryntirion on Salop Road.

Bryntirion, Salop Road.

Cyril enlisted with the 3rd Battalion, Montgomeryshire Yeomanry, which trained and supplied men for general service on the East Coast.

There is very little information available on Cyril's military service. He was living at 6 Christchurch Road, Bournemouth when he died on 8th January 1920. It is likely that he was suffering with respiratory problems and was there for the sea air. He was 19 years old.

Cyril is buried here at Christ Church.

'Abide with me'

Appendix a.   Acknowledgements

Photo credits:

Leonard Augustus Hedge: Site of United Counties Bank p. 12 – Charlie Bass. Brecon War Memorial p.14,15 – Charlie Bass.

Ernest Watkins: Freemasons Memorial Book p. 34 – Phil Addicott.

Joseph Ithel Jehu Davies: The Davies brothers p. 41 – Lilian Gilbert-Davies. Headstone p. 47 – Colin Rogers. Military medals p. 48 – Lilian Gilbert-Davies.

John Thomas & Edward Thomas: The Thomas brothers p. 67 & 100 – Bethan Pryce.

Harold Owen Davies & James Wilfred Davies: The Davies family p. 80 & 93 – Pamela MacDonald. Owen Davies & Trevor Davies p. 81 – Pamela MacDonald.

Rex Manford: Ribemont Communal Cemetery Extension p. 130 – Michael and Janet Bennett. Headstone p. 131 – Michael and Janet Bennett.

William Waring: Family leaving Buckingham Palace p. 139 – Jim Simister.

Research assistance:

My sincere gratitude to the families who gave me photographs and information to help me write the story of their relative – Alun Pryce, Bethan Pryce, Lilian Gilbert-Davies, Margaret Parker, Pamela MacDonald.

A very big thank you to Colin Rogers who is always so generous in sharing his extensive knowledge of old Welshpool. I am grateful to Roger L. Brown for sharing his local historic information. My sincere thanks go to the late Jim Simister and Claire Millington who leant me several books and artifacts that were very helpful in the research for this project. I am also grateful to Roy Claffey and the late Pryce Howells for their anecdotal information on Welshpool's past.

My thanks to Karen Woolley, Joy Hamer, Phil Addicott and James Hall for their assistance in researching the archive records especially in the early days of the project.

I am extremely grateful to the trustees of the Old Gentleman's Club, Welshpool, whose financial support greatly helped the publication to get this far. The Welshpool Branch - Royal Naval Association, The Welshpool Branch - The Royal Welch Fusiliers Comrades Association, and The Powysland Club have also kindly supported the printing of this book, for which I am very grateful. Without the support of these organisations printing this book would have been merely a dream.

Sources:

Ancestry - www.ancestry.co.uk

Find My Past - www.findmypast.co.uk

The Long, Long Trail - www.1914-1918.net

World War One Battlefields - www.ww1battlefields.co.uk

Lives of the First World War - www.livesofthefirstworldwar.iwm.org.uk

Commonwealth War Graves Commission - www.cwgc.org

Forces War Records - www.forces-war-records.co.uk

The Wartime Memories Project - www.wartimememoriesproject.com

The Great War 1914 – 1918 - www.greatwar.co.uk

Cymru WW1 - www.cymru1914.org

Canadian War Museum - www.warmuseum.ca

BBC - www.bbc.co.uk

Wikipedia - www.wikipedia.org

War Diaries published online.

The National Trust – www.nationaltrust.org.uk

Personalities of Welshpool Series, Welshpool Rotary Club.

The Historical Records of the Montgomeryshire Yeomanry 1909-1919, compiled by Colonel R.W. Williams Wynn C.B. DSO and Major W.N. Stable M.C.

Readers Digest, The War to End Wars 1914 – 18.

Disclaimer:

I have endeavoured to portray the facts within each story to be as correct as possible. I hope that no errors or omissions will come to light, if so, I sincerely apologise.

Appendix b.   Welshpool War Memorial

The Welshpool War Memorial, St. Mary's Churchyard.

Designed by Sir Aston Webb in 1921.

Appendix c.   The Poppy Trail

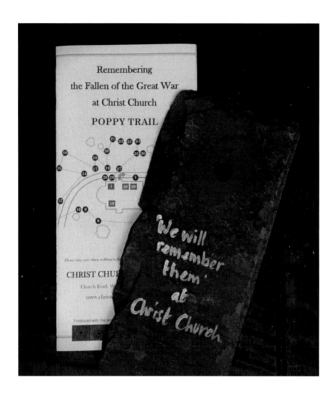

Each of the memorials featured in this book have been marked with a hand painted slate poppy and form a Poppy Trail. We have created a Poppy Trail leaflet to help guide you through the churchyard to see the memorials. The leaflet has been produced with the support of the Powys War Memorials Project, of which we are very grateful. The leaflet is free and is available from Christ Church Welshpool. Alternatively, you can download a copy by visiting:

www.powyswarmemorials.co.uk/walks-and-trails

Appendix d.   Christ Church Welshpool

One sunny afternoon, we stumbled across Christ Church, locked up and overgrown with ivy. It was for sale... intrigued an appointment was made to have a look inside and a seed of an idea was sown. A year later in 2003 we were the proud, if somewhat petrified, owners of Christ Church and our restoration journey began.

Designed by Thomas Penson in the early 1840's and previously owned by The Church in Wales, Christ Church closed in 1998. This Grade II* listed building stood empty with leaking roofs for 5 years. It seemed a travesty that this huge ornate and very special building was slowly deteriorating in this way. We had the vision of restoring Christ Church to its former glory, living in part of the building and reopening the nave to the public to honour its original function of bringing people together, therefore hopefully giving it a future.

We have converted the rear of the church into a family dwelling with our three sons, Owen, Fred and Victor. We have endeavoured to work as sympathetically as possible to the original design and building materials used. We are using approximately a quarter of the total area of the church as our private residence. Alongside the conversion works, we are continually undergoing repair works to the building, such as re-roofing, overhauling rainwater goods, re-pointing etc. We are still playing catch up on repair work inherited from when we first bought the building, but we are making slow progress.

We feel very strongly that Christ Church was designed for people and that accessibility should play an important role in its future. This would be of an advantage to the building as well as being beneficial to Welshpool, particularly as it would increase tourism within the town and widen the town's 'cultural scene'. The acoustics of the building are superb, and it would be a shame not to give the organ a new lease of life! Christ Church Welshpool operates as a not-for-profit organisation to ensure the building's future is protected and self-sustainable, with the overall aim to enable the public to continue to have access to this beautiful Victorian building.

Christ Church has become our life, not just our home. The process of its restoration has been both enlightening and fulfilling, if a little daunting and overwhelming at times. There are so many interesting threads here, such as the history, the people who connect to this place, the building's aesthetics, the churchyard and the stories it holds, along with the wildlife, all to be woven together to write the next chapter in the future of Christ Church.

Our progress can be followed on our website at www.christchurchwelshpool.co.uk

Karl & Natalie

Christ Church Welshpool

Church Road, Welshpool, Powys. SY21 7LN

Christ Church Welshpool